D1601111

SENSATIONAL
Sex

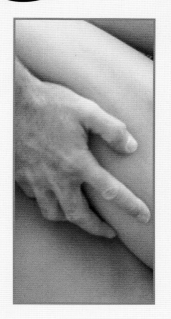

SENSATIONAL
Sex

Linda Sonntag

hamlyn

This edition first published in
Great Britain in 2002 by Hamlyn,
a division of Octopus Publishing Group
Ltd, 2–4 Heron Quays, London, E14 4JP

Distributed in the United States and
Canada by
Sterling Publishing Co., Inc.
387 Park Avenue South, New York,
NY 10016–8810

ISBN 0 600 60583 3
EAN 9780600605836

A CIP catalogue record of this book is
available from the British Library.

Printed in Hong Kong

The author has asserted her moral rights.

The material in this book has been
adapted from *Sensational Sex* previously
published by Hamlyn

Warning With the prevalence of AIDS
and other sexually transmitted diseases,
if you do not practise safe sex you are
risking both your health and that of
your partner.

CONTENTS

INTRODUCTION

Real sex is deeply committed sex. This means letting go, and giving and feeling 100 per cent, in both mind and body. *Sensational Sex* shows you how to raise your sexual awareness on every level, how to communicate it to your partner and experience new highs of emotion and sensation. Focusing in depth on the five senses, it will help you to tune into each one of them, to develop their potential and enjoy them to the full.

The idea behind this book is based on a modern adaptation of the ancient Indian practice of Tantra. The Tantrists are perhaps best remembered for weirdly contorted sexual positions that have no part in present-day life in the West, as they need years of yoga to perfect. But the Tantric philosophy of oneness and wholeness is as relevant today as it was then.

With your mind and all your senses fully attuned to your own and your partner's pleasure, sex becomes not only a physical delight but also a deeply spiritual and healing experience. Developing your sensual awareness will help you unlock your sexual power and transform your life with confidence and joy.

Sight

It starts with the eyes. One look and we are hooked! Or is there more to love at first sight than that? This chapter analyses the underlying forces governing our attraction to particular individuals, and reveals how we unconsciously send sexual signals to each other by our behaviour and the way we dress. It also explores ways in which we can exploit the sense of sight to enrich our sex lives – the tantalizing thrill of watching without touching.

FIRST IMPRESSIONS

What is it that makes two complete strangers fall in love at first sight; to feel a powerful kind of recognition before they have been given any information about each other or even heard a voice or an opinion? Is it a person's face or their physique? Or is it their clothes, posture or gestures? The answer is all of these, because they all add up to a presence that fits an individual's requirements for a potential partner on both a conscious and a subconscious level.

Most impressions are formed within approximately two minutes of first seeing someone. We collate all the information received, combine it with data already stored in a vast memory bank and come to conclusions about that person very quickly.

MAKING JUDGEMENTS

In reality most of us still make the mistake of 'judging a book by its cover'. Fat people are always assumed to be jolly; thin people are thought likely to be morose. Blonde women are seen to be more fun-loving than brunettes, while men who are balding have a reputation for being more virile than those with a full head of hair. These are just a few examples of the generalizations that continue to influence our thinking when dealing with others. In this way, however, we run the risk of limiting our chances of finding happiness.

We have only to stop and consider our past experience with relationships to remind ourselves of the complexity of human interaction. People often say of someone who has let them down in some way, 'I should have followed my gut instinct'. Conversely, many of us will have expressed the sentiment, 'I really didn't like him/her when we first met, but I have been pleasantly surprised on getting to know them better'. Yet in the face of this knowledge, we still rely on snap judgements.

However, we would be foolish if, in the interests of being open-minded in our encounters with others, we failed to heed a blatant piece of body language. For example, if someone walked towards us in the street brandishing a knife, we would not stop to weigh up the possibility that they might be on their way home to carve a roast joint. There are times when immediate judgement is called for, but equally there are times when we have more time for assessment. In social situations, we usually have a chance to make a judgement and also to review it.

ATTRACTION

The fact that you can look across a crowded room and be immediately attracted to an individual – a fleeting moment that could change the direction of your life – is both exciting and daunting, but is this just a chance happening? Is it as random as that? How much of what we see is coloured by our own unconscious experience, emotional background and expectations?

It may be that the person you are looking at fits a 'check-list' of desirable attributes in a potential partner that has evolved in your mind over time and through experience. You may also be unconsciously reacting to the positive way others around the stranger are responding.

Alternatively, a potential mate may have a look about them that reminds us of someone we have loved from afar, or loved and lost; perhaps it is the way they talk or flick their hair out of their eyes, or their choice of clothes or simply the way they stand. There is something comforting about being in a room of strangers and unexpectedly meeting someone with whom we feel unaccountably familiar. It may even be that the individual reminds us of a person who influenced us in our formative years, whether for good or bad. In the latter case, it is a well-documented fact that girls who were abused by their fathers often form relationships with men given to abusing women. Albeit self-destructive, their formative knowledge of sexual relationships includes such abuse and it is therefore expected.

EXPECTATIONS

'Expected' is a key word when it comes to love at first sight. Catching the eye of someone in a crowded room and making our assessment of them involves expecting certain things. Because they look smartly dressed, we may expect them to be

polite. Because they have dyed purple and orange hair, we may expect them to be wacky or free-thinkers. If politeness or free-thinking is on our 'check-list' of attraction, when we meet them and have a conversation that destroys these illusions the initial attraction goes out of the window. If our preconceptions are upheld when the person who caught our eye comes across to say hello, love has a chance to bloom.

EYE CONTACT

Although it is a cliché that the eyes are windows to the soul, it contains a strong element of truth. Talking to someone in dark glasses for any length of time can be disconcerting. Even though only their eyes are covered, it still somehow limits our ability to connect with the person.

We all respond to the way people use their eyes. A person who cannot maintain eye contact could be feeling very shy, nervous or guilty about something, whereas someone who stares is thought to be rude, hostile or even threatening. Yet prolonged eye contact where other body language is overtly open and friendly can be attractive. Eyes that narrow, often combined with a knitting of eyebrows, show anger and displeasure. Eyes opened wide can display enormous pleasure and excitement.

EYE ALLURE

Eyes can speak their own language of attraction. Eyes that flit away fleetingly then look back, especially if they are accompanied by a shy flutter of the eyelashes, can be a come-on. A slow blinking of eyes, coupled with a Madonna-like smile, can be sexually intriguing.

Sexual excitement manifests itself in the eyes in a direct physical response – in the dilation of the pupils. During the 18th century, Italian women would put drops of the plant belladonna in their eyes because it had the property of dilating the pupils, thus making them look sexy. Subdued lighting has the same effect, which is just one of the reasons why candlelight is romantic.

When we meet someone new, eye contact is the first interaction. We quickly scan their face, usually paying most attention to their eyes and mouth. Should they offer their hand, leaning forward very slightly, giving a firm but not uncomfortable shake, at the same time as tilting their head to one side and smiling with the mouth and eyes, we would probably feel at ease. If on the other hand they took a step backwards, held their head and neck stiffly and simply nodded to us with unblinking eyes and tight lips, most of us would feel very uncomfortable. Their body language is expressing no desire to have any interaction with us at all.

BODY LANGUAGE

It is estimated that at least 80 per cent of communication is taken up with non-verbal signals. When two people meet, if things proceed well, their body language reinforces their positive interaction. As they talk – perhaps a little hesitantly at first while they feel their way – they will keep eye contact for increasing periods of time. Their hand gestures become more expansive and, given time, may even become possessive. For example, a man who is talking to a woman on his left at a dinner table may, as the conversation heats up, twist to face her, placing his arm across the table as a barrier to the person on his right.

BREAKING DOWN BARRIERS

Similarly, when a newly introduced couple face each other at a bar, there is at first an invisible barrier between them which is gradually broached, perhaps by moving a glass across into the other's personal space. This may be followed by leaning closer or talking quietly, inviting the other person to move closer.

As the attraction grows, so the body language becomes more animated. They face each other with wide eyes, eyebrows raised, mouths open and smiling or laughing. Their heads lift back, revealing neck and throat. Arms become more relaxed and move away from protecting the body. They nod frequently, encouraging the other to continue to talk. They may even discuss others in the room in a critical way, aligning themselves as a couple. At the same time, they are finding out what it is that makes the other one approve or disapprove. Later, as the pair have got to know each other and the mood becomes more sensual, quieter more intimate talk begins with touching of hands, an arm around a waist, a kiss on the cheek and, finally, the first kiss on the mouth.

GENDER DIFFERENCES

When primitive society changed from a nomadic life of gathering fruits and berries to one more dependent on hunting game, the male body developed and evolved to cope with more strenuous requirements.

Modern-day man still reflects these changes. The male body is larger, taller and more muscular than the female. The skull and jaw are stronger to protect against attack. The male shoulders are broad, giving strength and load-bearing ability, and the chest is also broader, with a large lung capacity allowing for physical exertion. The arms and legs are more powerful to assist in carrying heavy loads and to enable faster running speeds. The male body, now as then, is geared to provide for and protect the human species.

The female body has evolved to facilitate child-bearing and is not built for the speed needed for hunting and fighting. The pelvis is wide and tilts back slightly to aid childbirth. Extra fat deposits on hips and thighs with a longer belly give the strength needed for carrying a foetus. Enlarged breasts and nipples have developed for the suckling of the young.

ADVERTIZING GENDER

Other differences in male and female sexual characteristics have nothing to do with evolution and past necessities. They are there simply to advertise the gender. The male body is usually hairier than the female's, although loss of head hair often leads to baldness later in life. The male Adam's apple is much more prominent than the female's and after puberty the voice is much deeper. The female body is generally fleshier than the male's, and overall more rounded in appearance, especially around the shoulders, breasts, buttocks and knees.

DRESS SENSE

At certain times in our history, fashion has accentuated the parts of the body that distinguish one sex from another. For men, the codpiece emphasized the crotch bulge and shoulder pads showed off brawny shoulders, whereas for women, the bustle highlighted the buttocks and corsets trimmed the waist while making the breasts more prominent. In contrast, during the 1920s, the androgynous dropped waists and flattened breast and buttock line did everything to conceal the female form as women gained an independence previously enjoyed only by men.

NAKEDNESS

The sight of your lover's naked body is an erotic turn-on, and a comfort, too. This is because nakedness signifies the stripping away not just of clothes but of all barriers between you, getting down to the simplest truths of your feelings for each other.

The first time you undress in front of each other, desire, curiosity and impatience may be spoiled by a fear of not looking quite right, perhaps too fat or too thin. Continually bombarded with images of bodies that are marketed as perfect, most of us feel physically inadequate at times. But the body is a house for the person within, and expresses the beauty and desirability of that individual in countless unique ways.

Take time to study the texture of your lover's skin and get to know its various markings, moles and scars. Look at the way the hair grows from your lover's brow. Follow the contours of their shoulders, chest, waist, buttocks and thighs until you know them by heart. Cherish the hands and the feet; wonder at the veins and bones, and marvel at the ear lobes and navel. Watch the way your lover moves. Carefully study your partner's genitals through the various stages of arousal.

Most couples take off all their clothes to make love, but sometimes, overtaken by urgency, half-undress may be all you can manage and the more exciting for that. A state of deliberate half-undress about the house as well as in bed can also prove tantalizing. Following Eastern customs, some women like to put on their jewellery for making love. If this appeals to you, bear in mind that in the rough and tumble anything sharp or hard can hurt, and earrings can get caught and pull painfully.

Sleeping together in the nude, bodies curled up like spoons or just touching, is a delicious sensation whether you have made love or not, but sometimes after a hot and sweaty session, skin

can stick together uncomfortably. A thin cotton or silk
chemise for one of you smoothes things out again without
losing the sensation of closeness that can be spoiled by bulky
nightwear. When you wake up in the night or in the early
morning, be sure not to miss the opportunity of studying your
lover's relaxed sleeping face.

OUTSIDE THE BEDROOM

Shared nudity need not be reserved for the bedroom. Enjoy the sight of your partner taking a bath or shower and watch the way they soap themselves or wash their hair. The bath is a good place to relax with a drink and talk about the day's events. Instead of putting on fresh clothes, just slip into a dressing gown to eat your evening meal. It is very appealing to see your partner at the table so nearly naked and ready for bed. Or strip off and eat naked in front of the fire, lying on the sofa and feeding each other like the Ancient Greeks and Romans used to do. Plan a naked picnic in a remote wood or moored in a rowing boat, or in a secluded cove – somewhere private where you can swim and make love afterwards with the sun and the air on your skin. Try dancing in the nude, or undressing each other as you go. Try kissing and having sex while you are dancing.

NUDISM

Some people find that informal nudity around the house is not enough for them. Nudist camps, where group activities are carried out in the buff, may provide the ideal solution. Some of these pursuits performed naked, such as playing crazy golf or wheeling a trolley round a supermarket, seem bizarre to some but can be appealing and highly enjoyable for others. Nudist colonies are places for families, but if you want to join one, do not try to force your children to take part. Growing children often find their parents' nudity disturbing – how would you feel about your own parents in the nude? Also, do not try to persuade your partner to join in if he or she feels reticent about public nakedness or uneasy about your motives. To undress or not to undress should always be a personal choice.

WATCHING

Most of us are turned on by erotic situations. It could be hearing a couple making love on the other side of a wall, or accidentally discovering a pair of lovers in a wood enjoying a sexual encounter. How would you feel if you found your lover masturbating? Would you be shocked, or angry that you were not enough for them? Or would it arouse you? Your response might be a combination of all of these.

It should be said that masturbation, or self-pleasuring, in no way discounts the love and understanding a close couple have for each other. It is more of an extension of that, and it can be an even greater step towards sexual ecstasy if you are prepared to share it. If either you or your partner are having difficulties in achieving orgasm together, it could be an educational experience – one that will enrich your sex life thereafter. Watching is one sure way of finding out what makes your lover melt.

Though sex aids hold no interest for many women, some find the insertion of a dildo, or the use of a vibrator, tremendously exciting. A lubricant jelly specially designed for use on the genital area, or an oil such as almond oil, stimulates the labia and clitoris, allowing the fingers to glide with ease, helping to release any initial tension felt by being watched. Alternatively, the use of a blindfold can help you to stay focused and remove any distraction felt by your lover's presence in the room.

FEMALE MASTURBATION

Women may start masturbating later in life than men, but by the time they are ready to masturbate in front of their lover, they have usually discovered the most enjoyable way to reach orgasm. Some women like to lie on their front, others on their back.

Some prefer their legs wide open, while others enjoy the increased pressure of their closed thighs. Whichever position is favoured, glide the hands softly over the belly, move the fingers through the pubic hair and touch the lips of the vagina. Move slowly and purposefully – this is not a race against time. Lubricate the whole of the vulva, opening up the lips like the petals of a flower. When you are ready, use your finger or fingers to experiment with different strokes – the middle finger has more strength and control. A hardening and swelling of the clitoris, together with a flush of moist warmth in the vagina, is the beginning of an ecstatic sexual journey. Having found the perfect rhythm for you, maintain it and increase the arousal. At this point, you may enjoy caressing the whole area around

the genitals, or the nipples, with your other hand. Some women like to insert a dildo to intensify their orgasm.

MALE MASTURBATION

Male masturbation was once considered a sin; something shameful to hide away. It should be seen as a step towards self-acceptance and, in the context of being watched by your lover, a wonderful offering up of your inner secrets. Take your time. Consume yourself in sexual fire.

First run your hands over your body, touching all the parts that you find sensual. Move down slowly, over your belly, and run your fingers through your pubic hair. Slide your hand down your groin and stroke the perineum (the area between the anus and the scrotum), the scrotum and testicles. Massaging the perineum stimulates the prostate into sexual arousal. This move is especially useful if you are someone who needs a longer massage for arousal.

Try sitting with your back against a wall for support so that you can touch these areas more easily. The faster you stroke, and the stronger the pressure on the perineum, the quicker the arousal will be. If the anus is a part of your pleasure, oil it well and insert a finger very gently. Make sure your nails are clean and short, since the lining of the anus is quite fragile. Pay attention to hygiene afterwards.

Lubricate the whole of the genital area, including the penis. Handle the penis gently at first. Holding it with one hand, run the fingers of the other from the base up the shaft, across the ridge to the tip. Move the hand up and down and all around, caressing and pulling. Experiment with different movements and pressure. Pay special attention to the sensitive head of the penis and the frenulum. Spread extra lubricant lightly over the tip if needed and continue your chosen method of stimulation with an insistent rhythm, building up to the point of orgasm.

WATCHING OTHERS

Many people get erotic pleasure from watching others have sex as well as from doing it themselves. Women can get just as aroused by sexual images as men, provided they are not intended to degrade or hurt. If looking with your partner at pictures or videos of people making love turns you on, then introduce it as an occasional novelty into your sexual playtime. Use it as a means to more openness between you, to finding out more about each other's daydreams. Often words act as a more potent stimulus to the imagination than images, so you could take it in turns to read each other an erotic bedtime story, or even make up a story that you know will turn on your partner. Mental fantasies are also much more fluid than the celluloid variety, and the plots and acting in many blue movies are so unconvincing that they are more likely to cause boredom and snorts of ridicule than excitement. Of course, if you feel pornography violates your sense of privacy, then it is not for you.

Someone who gets kicks from secretly watching other people have sex, but not from doing it themselves, is a voyeur. Other people who do enjoy having sex themselves also like

watching couples make love, and this too is a form of voyeurism. In some parts of the world, sex-watching is considered a natural act, particularly in an initiation ceremony. In this context, sex is a public act that is witnessed with pleasure and without embarrassment by other members of the tribe or even of the same family. Still, watching sex is bound to turn making love into a performance and destroy its intimacy. Some people enjoy this and others definitely do not. Make sure you and your partner are both ready for it before you try it, and do not do it if only one of you wants to join in. Involving other people in your sexual partnership, at whatever level, can cause jealousy and insecurities that are hard to eradicate.

WATCHING YOURSELVES

Many people who would draw the line at watching, others gain a lot of pleasure from watching themselves. The advantage of having a large mirror in the bedroom is that you can see what you can normally only feel and imagine. Both of you can watch each other's face and genitals at the same time – something that is usually impossible. It is also a great boost to the confidence to see how radiant you look while making love.

Of course, some people find it off-putting to have their privacy intruded upon by their own reflections. They say mirrors blow open the intimacy of a bedroom and make it feel more like a shopping mall. As with everything else in sex, you should only do it if both you and your lover like it, but there is no harm in trying this one out to see.

DRESSING UP FOR SEX

Sexy clothes reveal as much as they conceal about the personality of the wearer as well as their body. Wearing clothes that hug contours and emphasize the figure is one way in which both men and women can send sexual signals. Dressing up for sex in fantasy clothes is something that appeals to people as a way of playing out parts of their personality that they do not normally exercise.

Women usually enjoy wearing clothes that make them feel sexy and get a good response from their partner, but sometimes there might be a niggling fear that the man in your bed is making love to the stockings and suspenders rather than to you. If you do dress up, make sure it is light-hearted and fun for both of you. Fantasies are for playtime only and should not be carried back into everyday life. If a man enjoys the feel of his partner's underwear against his own skin, it is not fair to accuse him at the breakfast table of being a transvestite. All that will do is break his trust and reinforce inhibitions. Similarly, the aggressions and disappointments of your relationship should not be acted out in a fantasy situation, which requires only playing at emotions and needs to be regarded more on the level of a saucy dream. Real anger and violence will shatter the dream and could do serious harm to a partner whom you have deliberately put in a vulnerable position.

SEXY SHOES

Sexy shoes are an essential part of dressing up. Delicate, strappy sandals combined with varnished toenails; exotic evening slippers and mules designed for the boudoir rather than the pavement; red shoes for dancing in; fierce leather thigh boots and stiletto heels all deserve a place in your fantasy wardrobe.

Why is it that many men are turned on by the sight of a woman in high heels? For some, it is because they like the idea of being treated severely by a tall woman in aggressively spiked shoes. It takes them back to a childhood where sexual thrills were associated with punishment. But for most, it is because the heeled shoe gives the female body a more curvaceous silhouette. To balance against the forward thrust produced by the heel, a woman has to arch her back, which means pushing forward with her belly and breasts. This also has the effect of emphasizing the waist and buttocks. The calf muscle tightens as the heel is raised, creating yet another curve. The teetering walk of a woman on stilettos throws all the body curves into sinuous action and suggests vulnerability as well as sensuality.

There are other aspects to shoes, apart from their heels, that have sexual appeal. The act of pushing the foot into the shoe is in itself a sexual symbol. It is no coincidence that this is how Cinderella was united with her prince. The feet of the ugly sisters were too big for the slipper, and in one version of the story a sister cuts off her big toe in an attempt to make it fit – a clear reference to castration.

The toe of a shoe is a phallic symbol, made obvious in such shoes as the *poulaine*, a man's shoe of the Middle Ages with a toe so long it had to be stuffed with moss to keep it erect. It was sometimes curled up and back and chained to the ankle. A modern woman's peep-toe sandal has a similar sexual significance.

Shoes and slippers edged with fur or decorated with a fluffy pompon are symbols of the vagina and pubic hair. The fact that Cinderella's slipper was made incongruously of glass is due to a fault in the transcription of the original manuscript, where it is described not as *de verre* (of glass) but *de vair* (of fur), which would have been more symbolically appropriate as well as easier to wear.

Shoes with straps and buckles have connotations of bondage, while shoes that display the arch of a woman's foot or the 'cleavage' of her toes are reminiscent of corsets that both reveal and conceal the breasts. While few men are serious shoe fetishists, the sexual potency of the shoe works on all of us and is there to be used and enjoyed.

Taste

Let your passion rip in this chapter, and savour the essence of your partner to the full. Learn how to get the most out of kissing, then graduate to giving your partner an all-over-body mouth massage by licking, sucking, nibbling and blowing. Develop the control and sensitivity of your tongue and lips still further, and sample the ultimate intimate pleasures of oral sex.

KISSING

The contact of another's lips as an act of greeting or farewell, friendship, love and sexual desire is a common custom in many societies, though not all. Although Japanese erotic literature as early as the ninth century expounds on the delights of kissing, many Eastern cultures lacked such a custom until it was introduced to them by Westerners. Up to the late 19th century, certain Chinese communities recoiled with horror at mouth-to-mouth kissing, as if witnessing a form of cannibalism.

In primitive societies, mothers would chew food to make it digestible for their babies and pass the pulp mouth-to-mouth. The young would search with their tongues for the food, so penetrative oral contact associated with love and caring was an early association.

Psychologists and anthropologists who have analysed the act of mouth-to-mouth kissing have theorized that it is a carry-over of the primitive eating habit, involving taking into the self anything that is nourishing and desirable. Modern-day lovers often feel the overwhelming need to consume each other through sucking, kissing, thrusting with the tongue and even biting. The ancient Egyptian word for kiss translates as 'to eat', and indeed the senses involved in kissing are the same ones used when eating – taste, smell and touch.

LEARN THE ART

Kissing, like all other aspects of lovemaking, is something for couples to explore and develop. Given the variety of lip and mouth sizes, it is simply not the case that just because you find each other physically attractive, your mouths will fit together. If they do, it could be a bonus of nature or it might be that one or both of you are great kissers. The art of kissing is something that

can be learnt. Violent thrusting of the tongue down the throat, pressing the lips down hard in the misconstrued belief that pressure equals passion, and sloppy, loose wet kisses are all ways not to kiss anyone, let alone begin a potential sexual relationship.

WAYS TO A SENSUAL MOUTH

Oral hygiene is of great importance. Clean teeth and gums and frequent check-ups with a dentist will ensure a foundation for sweet breath. Tobacco stains and the smell of stale tobacco are not pleasant when both partners smoke, but if only one partner puffs, it is doubly important that he or she pays special attention to using mouthwashes and herbal mouth sweeteners.

Spicy foods, especially garlic, should be given a miss unless you eat them together – particularly in the early flowering of a relationship. Chewing parsley or watercress, or sucking mints, will help in an emergency.

Sensual lips are soft. They can be kept smooth and crack-free with lip balms and creams during extreme weather. Flavoured lip balms can add a tantalizing appeal and do not smudge or stain, as some lipsticks can, in the heat of the moment.

Men with moustaches and/or beards should keep them trimmed – hairs tickling, or worse still, prickling your lover's nose when kissing her can be extremely off-putting. Remember that sporting a beard does not preclude the use of subtle aftershave or men's lotions, although your own clean smell can be just as erotic.

PRACTICE MAKES PERFECT

Too often, kissing is neglected in the urgency of a more complete union of the genitals. Yet leisurely kissing can be almost as sexually overwhelming and most tenderly fulfilling. In situations where pre-marital sex is frowned upon, or under-age but sexually aware virgin couples resist 'going all the way', hours are spent in sensual kissing. Conversely, couples in long-standing relationships whose intimate feelings have faded will hardly ever kiss during sexual intercourse, highlighting their lost intimacy.

So, kissing can be a pleasurable erotic experience on its own, or highly arousing foreplay, but where to begin? Make sure you are both comfortable. The back-breaking, neck-bending swoop down may look romantic in films but is not sustainable. Start by looking at your partner – really looking at them. You are about to kiss them in a way you would never kiss a passing acquaintance. Cup their face with firm hands. Flutter kisses over the forehead, down the nose and lightly on each eyelid. Ease their body towards you – kissing is heightened with loving caresses. Press your lips softly against theirs and slowly suck first the top then the bottom lip, parting them gently.

Slide your tongue languidly over your own mouth from corner to corner, then repeat the movement across the lips of your partner. Flick your tongue inside their mouth, feeling for the response of theirs. Increase the pressure of thrusting the tongue and lips and vary the kissing techniques in accordance with your partner's response.

BODY KISSING

Just as the lips and mouth send out chemical signals to the genitals, so too can other areas of the body. The skin, with its millions of nerve endings, is a feast of sensuality just waiting to be awakened. Certain parts of the body are almost always accessible for kissing – try kissing the back of your partner's neck, ears and upper arms. The hands, too, are sensitive areas that are too often overlooked. Feel free to spontaneously reach out for your partner, perhaps in the kitchen or when passing on the stairs. There should be no set rules about the time and place for sexual contact in a warm and sensuous relationship.

When you can, set aside time to spend together. For a mood-setting prelude, try a luxurious bath scented with relaxing or stimulating oils (see page 56). Take the telephone off the hook and move into a warm room. Candles give enough light and cast deliciously erotic shadows on naked skin. You could burn incense or play soft music. Place fresh food within easy reach that can be laid on the body and plucked with the lips or licked off with the tongue, without being too intrusive or messy. In short, set a scene that is calming and abandoned.

WHERE TO START

Run your hands lightly over the area you are about to kiss. The back and buttocks are particularly sensitive. Kiss the back of the neck and work downwards. Make full use of your lips, tongue and nose. Lick and nibble with your mouth and nuzzle gently with your nose. Breathe in your lover's smell. Pay attention and determine from their reaction the parts of their body that are particularly responsive. Avoid those that are obviously ticklish and concentrate on areas not normally touched in day-to-day life – the inner thighs, the backs of the knees, the curve of the

stomach. There are no taboo areas. Men and women can enjoy having their nipples licked, sucked and kissed. Body kissing is a way of connecting with the inner person through intimacy, and can be rewarding in its own right. But if it is something you both enjoy, body kissing is an ideal precursor to oral sex.

ORAL SEX

Oral sex is possibly the most intimate of all sexual practices. Some people worry about the open vulnerability of oral sex, which demands complete trust and confidence from both partners. Men especially may fear the penis being bitten inadvertently. Another common fear held by both sexes is that their partner, or they themselves, will not enjoy the sight, taste or smell of this intimacy. There is no reason why, given care and attention, these fears cannot be allayed.

When about to experiment with any aspect of sexual activity that has not arisen before as part of a progressive occurrence, there is nothing wrong with discussing it. Sex manuals and videos can be very useful in raising discussions about an issue that could enrich both partners' sex life. Men and women can be equally guilty of not asking their partners to try something they want to share because they are worried that it might seem strange or deviant in some way. Needless to say, this is not the time to pressurize someone into doing something over which they feel they have no control. Any discussion should begin by asking what the other person feels about it. Do they have strong feelings one way or another? If not, would they be prepared to try it out? The aim in all sexual activity should be for both partners to feel confident about giving and receiving pleasure.

As with all aspects of making love, the body should be clean, but this is especially important when it comes to oral sex. The odour of fresh sexual juices can be a turn-on for many, but unwashed stale odours can be offensive. Uncircumcised men should pay attention to the area under the foreskin, which can be a breeding place for germs if not regularly sluiced. If either of you has an infection of the mouth, throat or genitals, it is advisable to wait until this has cleared up before having oral sex.

Complete relaxation is necessary for pleasurable oral sex. It should never be undertaken in a hurried or forceful way. Some lovers advocate position 69, in which the couple lie head to genitals so that oral sex can be performed simultaneously. Others find the experience so overwhelming that they need to concentrate on their own enjoyment individually.

HOW TO PLEASE HER

The woman's partner should begin by either caressing and kissing her body from the mouth down, or lying between her legs and first kissing, licking or nuzzling her legs and inner thighs, using their hands to stroke the outsides of her thighs. Move your hands across her groin and caress the pubic hair

softly. Her thighs will part further with increased excitement, revealing the outer and inner lips of the vagina. Working slowly and using fingers if necessary, part the hair and locate the clitoris. Lightly flick the tongue back and forth, in and around the area. Suck the tip gently. If the sheath protecting it is raised, the sensation may be too intense. Proceed slowly, perhaps inserting a finger into the vagina to simulate penetration. Then, lubricating the clitoral area with saliva, continue lapping with the tongue. Vary speed and position according to her response.

Like the penis, the clitoris will engorge and swell with arousal, but the clitoris is more complex – one false move of the tongue in the early stages can put the sexual build-up back to the beginning. If a particular rhythm is working, continue to maintain it, unless response dictates otherwise, to the point of orgasm. If the excitement drops a little, caress the body in other places, then return and build up the momentum again.

HOW TO PLEASE HIM
The man's partner should begin by kissing and caressing other parts of his body, slowly and tantalizingly moving towards the target area. Touch and kiss his inner thighs, testicles and pubic hair before reaching for the penis. Taking it in one or both hands, lightly slide the tongue along the base to the head of the shaft. Flick the tongue over the top and down the underside, paying attention to the sensitive penis head and frenulum. Repeat the procedure, using the lips in a gentle kissing motion.

Slip the tip of the head into your mouth, taking care to guard the teeth with your lips. Suck the head in deeper while caressing the rest of the shaft with sensual movements of the fingers. Suck the head while simultaneously working the tongue around, above and below the ridge. The man should

not thrust if his partner has expressed fears of feeling choked. However, a slow rhythmic rocking should be acceptable. If in any doubt, the man should remain still while his partner moves her head up and down. Alternatively, she can use the tongue and lips while applying friction to the shaft manually.

Fellatio can be done to the point of ejaculation. However, some women find the idea repellent. This can be overcome by stopping and bringing your partner to climax by hand or switching to intercourse. However, many women enjoy bringing their man to climax in the mouth and like the taste of the warm fluid. Some even believe semen to have health benefits.

APHRODISIACS

Aphrodisiacs, named after Aphrodite, the Greek goddess of love, are drugs reputed to excite lust. They may also be taken to stave off exhaustion or heighten pleasure during sex.

The Greeks favoured eggs, honey, snails and shellfish such as mussels and crabs, while one Arabian recipe from *The Perfumed Garden* recommends a glass of very thick honey, 20 almonds and 100 pine nuts to be taken nightly for three nights on retiring. Other recipes were to be applied externally. In order 'to increase the dimensions of small members and make them splendid', the author of *The Perfumed Garden* advised rubbing the penis with melted fat from the hump of a camel, bruised leeches, asses' members and even hot pitch.

The Chinese were more scientific in their approach. They measured and blended the powdered roots of plants, then gave them colourful names such as 'the bald chicken drug'. This drug got its name when a septuagenarian paid so much attention to his wife after taking it that she could no longer sit or lie down. He was forced to throw the remains of the drug out into the yard, where it was gobbled up by the cockerel. The cock jumped on a hen straight away, and mated with her for several days without interruption, all the while pecking at her head to keep his balance, until the chicken was completely bald, whereupon the cockerel fell off. The proud inventor of the drug claimed that if it was taken three times a day for 60 days, a man would easily keep 40 women satisfied.

HORNY

Another Chinese recipe was 'deer horn potion', made of powdered antler, which was designed to prevent impotence. Horns of all kinds have long been thought to possess aphrodisiac properties because of their obvious phallic shape; and continuing belief in the potency of rhinoceros horn has brought the African rhinoceros to the brink of extinction. In fact, the original phallic horn belonged to the mythical unicorn, a wild, white horse-like creature from whose forehead protruded a long horn with a red tip and magical powers.

This heavy symbolism has fuelled centuries of demand for aphrodisiacs made of horn, which consists of hard, fibrous tissue similar to hair and nails. Like them, rhino horn contains the protein keratin, together with the minerals sulphur, calcium and phosphorus. The addition of these essential elements to a poor diet might improve vigour, but a cheese sandwich would do just as well. The only additional consequence of using powdered rhino horn is to deplete the rhinoceros population still further.

SOPORIFICS

At the other end of the scale from the excitants are the soporifics. These are drugs that induce drowsiness and languor – even euphoria – in which sexual inhibitions melt away. The most commonly used and socially acceptable of these is alcohol. However, alcohol 'provokes the desire but takes away the performance', as Macbeth's porter points out, and the after-effects of too much drink are well known.

FOOD OF LOVE

On a more everyday theme, eating or drinking huge amounts is not wise if seduction is on your mind. Sharing small portions of delicious food, on the other hand, can be a relaxing and sensual experience – watch your lover peel a fig, or hold a spear of asparagus tantalizingly to the lips.

Cooking a meal together can be an enjoyable way to begin a wonderful evening. Part of the fun of making an aphrodisiac meal lies in the planning and mutual anticipation of the results. Sexually stimulating dishes should always look good and be served with style, whether eaten on a rug in a wood, in front of the fire, in bed, in the bath or by candlelight at the kitchen table. Let your imagination run wild, outside the normal, everyday rules of preparing and eating meals.

For example, the meals do not have to be well balanced affairs, served with green vegetables or eaten at a particular time of the day. You can drink kir at four in the morning, slide down a few oysters with a glass of Champagne mid-afternoon, or snack off a rich dessert for breakfast, if you so choose. The idea is to break out of the mould and do exactly as you like when you like. Eating aphrodisiac foods is part of the pleasure of being free to experiment with sensation.

Smell

Our natural body perfume is a total turn-on. We wash it away and we disguise it with artificial scents, but it is the ultimate chemistry of attraction. This chapter explores the scent of sex – our pheromones and the vital part they play in our sexual encounters. But natural scents other than our own can be used to positive effect in lovemaking. For instance, you can use aromatherapy to create a seductive atmosphere and induce a state of relaxed arousal.

THE SCENT OF SEX

Smell is the fastest of the five senses – it takes us a mere half second to distinguish which of the 10,000 smells logged in our brains is currently being wafted under our nose. But exactly how we do this has not yet been discovered.

The part of the brain that deals with the sense of smell is the limbic area. In primitive times, the sense of smell was far more important and thus better used than it is today. Our distant ancestors needed to rely on smell – of both their enemies and their prey – for survival. Today, our sense of smell still helps us recognize danger, for example something burning or bad food, but is more often used for pleasure, or simply not at all. On our bodies and in our homes, we mask a multitude of subtle, natural smells with artificial ones. Also, as mankind has evolved, the functions of the primitive brain, in which smell was so important, have expanded to include emotions, sexual behaviour, cognitive thought, creativity, memory, hunger and thirst, and body temperature. This explains why our sense of smell is so intimately involved with all of these things.

PHEROMONES

Pheromones are natural secretions that mark the identity of living creatures. A moth can detect a mate fluttering in a garden miles away. Even a snail can find its way home by identifying the trails of other snails. But humans largely ignore the smell of their mates. We use perfume, aftershave and deodorant to disguise our natural sweaty aromas. This is a great pity, because however well suited to someone you feel yourself to be, only the scent of their skin and the smell of their sweat will tell you the truth. If you have ever buried your head in your lover's shirt to recapture their presence, you will know that this is so.

AROMATHERAPY

'Fill the tent … with a variety of different perfumes, amber, musk, and all sorts of scents, as rose, orange flowers, jonquils, jasmine, hyacinth, carnation and other plants. This done, have placed there several gold censers filled with green aloes, ambergris and so on. Then fix the hangings so that nothing of these perfumes can escape out of the tent. Then, when you find the vapour strong enough to impregnate water, sit down on your throne, and send for the prophetess to come and see you in the tent, where she will be alone with you. When you are thus together there, and she inhales the perfumes, she will delight in the same, all her bones will be relaxed in a soft repose and finally she will be swooning. When you see her thus far gone, ask her to grant you her favours; she will not hesitate to accord them.'

This is an extract from one of the most famous Arab erotic books, *The Perfumed Garden*, which was dedicated to the art of using scents in seduction. The Arabs were pioneers in the art of perfumery. They discovered how to extract potent essential oils from aromatic plants and to take civetone and muskone from the sex glands of live civet cats and musk deer. Today, you can try out seductive scents on your lover at home by learning the art of aromatherapy – using the oils of aromatic plants as a complete treatment for physical and mental wellbeing. These powerful oils can be used for a sensual massage, in the bath and to scent the bedroom via an oil burner.

The practice of aromatherapy is thousands of years old and was probably first employed systematically in China. The ancient Indian medical discipline, the Ayurveda, which is still

alive today, also uses plant essences to combat infection, soothe inflammation and relieve tension and depression.

It is still not known how essential oils actually work. The volatile molecules of which the molecules are composed dissolve in oil or water. When released into the air, they are inhaled in minute water droplets. At the top of the nose, they are intercepted by the olfactory nerve cells and from this point their messages are transmitted to the brain. When rubbed into the skin, the aromatic molecules are absorbed into the body through its natural oil or sebum.

SCENT SEDUCTION

Professional aromatherapists design treatments specifically for each individual, but for home use, you can select certain oils based on their commonly acknowledged properties (see page 58). Some are known to lift the spirits, while others calm them. Oils that combine both effects are particularly good for inducing a state of relaxed arousal.

USING ESSENTIAL OILS

Essential oils can be administered in several ways. For massage (see pages 100–1), the oils must be diluted in a neutral carrier oil. Never apply neat essential oil to the skin, since it could cause severe skin irritation. You can buy oils that are ready diluted, but if you use the concentrated essence, it needs to be mixed in the proportion of 1:50 with a carrier oil such as almond, apricot, hazelnut or safflower oil. Always store essential oils in tightly capped dark glass bottles in a cool place. They are highly volatile and evaporate if exposed to heat, light or air.

The diluted oils can be applied to the face and body, and rubbed or massaged into the skin. The base of the spine and the back of the neck are good application points for the relief of tension. You can inhale essential oils directly from the bottle, or add one or two drops to a bowl of hot water, bend your head over it and drape a towel over you and the bowl to keep in the steam. This is effective when using peppermint or eucalyptus oil to relieve breathing problems. Another way to enjoy the oils is to add ten drops to a bath. Make sure the water temperature suits you both, and share a long, relaxing soak.

To make a room or body spray, add about five drops of essential oil to 600 ml (1 pint) water and use the fragrant water in a spray mist bottle. To scent a room, you can also add a few drops of oil to a bowl of water near a radiator, or sprinkle some drops of oil on to a ring specially designed to fit a standard light-bulb. An oil burner with a shallow dish set over a candle is another option. Water is poured into the dish, to which you add drops of your favourite oil then light the candle. The heat vaporizes the oil, dispersing the seductive aroma into the air.

ESSENTIAL OILS FOR VAPORIZING

Essential oils are wonderful when warmed in an oil burner – the particles diffuse through the air and surround you with delicious aromas. (See pages 100–1 for oils for massage.)

Basil A warm, peppery smell, evocative of Italian sunshine. Basil lifts the spirits and clears the mind.

Bergamot This scent comes from the peel of an orange-like fruit. It fights infection. Do not apply it to the skin before sunbathing or using a sunbed, since it can cause blotchy pigmentation.

Cedarwood A warm, woody, violet smell. This is good for the hair, skin and urinary tract.

Camomile A warm, aromatic scent, which is relaxing, calming and mildly sedative. This is a good oil for relieving stress.

Clary sage A nutty, flowery scent. This gives a real sense of euphoria and is good as an aphrodisiac and for fatigue.

Clove Warm spicy scent with anaesthetic and antiseptic properties.

Cypress A fresh, woody smell, which is relaxing and good for the circulation.

Eucalyptus An antiseptic and good for breathing problems. It stimulates the nervous system and clears the head.

Frankincense A spicy, woody aroma. It acts well on the emotions with a relaxing, rejuvenating and uplifting effect. A good aphrodisiac.

Geranium A floral scent. Geranium oil is a tonic, sedative and antiseptic, and balances the complexion and relieves anxiety. It also has aphrodisiac properties.

Jasmine Rich, exotic and sensual, jasmine lifts the mood and is used in classic perfumes. Highly regarded for its aphrodisiac effect.

Juniper A woody, fresh scent. Juniper is stimulating and relaxing, good for stress, fatigue and lack of energy. It is also an aphrodisiac.

Lavender A familiar floral fragrance. A stimulant, a relaxant, lavender is also antiseptic and an aphrodisiac.

Lemon A bittersweet, citrus scent. Refreshing and stimulating, lemon is also an antiseptic and astringent.

Lemongrass A lemony aroma, good for excessive sweating and migraines, and is also refreshing in the bath.

Marjoram A rich herbal aroma; soothes migraines and relieves insomnia.

Neroli From the flowers of the orange tree, neroli is relaxing and calming.

Orange A characteristic warm, citrus scent that is uplifting and refreshing.

Patchouli A seductive, oriental aroma, patchouli is a well-known aphrodisiac.

Peppermint It invigorates, refreshes, numbs pain and clears the head. Good for fatigue, headaches and PMS. It also lifts depression.

Pine A fresh, resinous smell; refreshing and antiseptic.

Rose A heady, floral scent. Rose is both a tonic and an aphrodisiac. It is beneficial for ageing skin, and improves circulation and breathing.

Rosemary A strong, resinous aroma, good for fatigue, depression and aches and pains.

Rosewood A spicy and refreshing essence which enlivens the spirits.

Sandalwood A musky scent which enhances sexual awareness, acting as both a sedative and a stimulant.

Tea tree A strong medicinal smell; excellent for cuts, burns and rashes.

Thyme A strong yet delicate aroma, good for fatigue, anxiety and headaches. A powerful antiseptic, it is used in gargles and to treat skin inflammation.

Ylang ylang An exotic, Far Eastern scent used as a love potion. It is very effective on the emotions as both a stimulant and a sedative.

Touch

Touch is a simple, eloquent form of communication – affirmative, reassuring, healing, comforting and essential. This chapter shows you how to use touch to express a whole range of feelings in a relationship, from conveying everyday tenderness as a prelude to sexual contact, to exploring different positions for sex, depending on your mood.

TENDERNESS

In a loving sexual relationship, touch is of vital importance. It is the sense we explore most luxuriously in bed, but the one that is sadly most often missing outside the bedroom. Does touching your partner always lead to sex? Do you avoid touching unless you're going to make love? Or are your bodies so at ease together that touching is just another way of communicating all sorts of shades of love? Do you snuggle, nuzzle, cuddle, hug, squeeze, push, wrestle, tickle? Are you physical? Are you tender?

In a caring relationship, tenderness can easily melt into sensuality and then to sexuality. But sexuality can always be held in check with a promise to satisfy it later, at a more convenient time. However, many women complain that their partners find touching without sex impossible, embarrassing, even a waste of time.

WHY MEN AND WOMEN ARE DIFFERENT

In the days when we all lived in caves, men were the hunters and protectors, and women the nurturers and carers. The emotions that developed to cope with these roles had to be different. Men needed to be hard and aggressive in order to survive. The physical contact they engaged in most was likely to be rough. But women, whose job it was to raise the next generation, couldn't afford not to be tender.

Today, male and female roles are not so clearly defined. Modern-day man contributes to the rearing of children far more than his ancestors did. But this change has taken place so recently in the long history of humankind that it hasn't really had time to settle into the male psyche, and make tenderness, touching, caring and listening part of the average male's natural make-up. Most women would claim that inwardly, things

haven't changed that much. Many men are aware that they miss out by not exploring the 'feminine' side of their nature. Accordingly, men's groups are increasingly common, where men gather together to talk on an emotional level instead of competitively, to share problems with one another and get in touch with their feelings. Of course it isn't every man's idea of fun to bare his inner self to his mates. But at least these 'new men' are trying to grow. It's the less communicative types, the

ones who just don't express their feelings to anyone, by touch or word, who are most likely to suffer from stress and the illnesses it causes.

The male body, with its strong and powerful frame, was built for action. When primitive man went out hunting for food, danger was constantly in the air. With each crisis, adrenalin pumped round his body and the choice was 'fight or flight' – our ancestor had to spring into action to save his skin. In the last few years of his long history on the planet, this same male animal finds himself shackled, perhaps to a desk, or another routine job in which decisions involve small tasks like pressing buttons instead of big actions like attacking or running. But the hormones coursing round his body are the same, and so are the feelings of danger. 'Will I lose my client/the contract/my job?' There is no physical release available from the great frustrations of the modern workplace. You can't run and hide, and you can't punch the boss. The adrenalin pumps, but the body is forced to sit still, and the consequences can be mental and physical illness.

Men who are not used to expressing their feelings therefore suffer a double disadvantage. At home, their relationship may drift into coolness. At work, they are faced with stress that could build into a life-threatening disease.

TOUCHING IS HEALING

Touch can open up the way to greater self-expression. Massage can bring relief from stress. A loving sexual relationship gives both partners the chance to redress imbalances between them. If it's good in bed, you can make it work out of bed too. Cuddling doesn't have to lead to sex and it doesn't have to be a sign of clinginess. It can express simple comfort and closeness.

HEALTHY SEX

A fulfilling sexual relationship can help boost good health, but sex and health are also connected in other ways that require serious consideration. The two main areas of concern are contraception and protection against sexually transmitted diseases (STDs), especially AIDS.

AIDS is at present an incurable condition that is usually fatal in the long term. It is transmitted by having unprotected sex with someone who is infected with HIV, the AIDS virus. As there are no immediate symptoms of the disease, it is not possible to tell who has already contracted it. This means that unprotected sex with any new partner carries a risk. The most effective way to protect yourself from the HIV virus is to use a condom every time you have sex. Some couples who do not wish to use a condom decide to take an AIDS test to make sure they are both clear of the virus.

HOW TO USE A CONDOM

Condoms come ready-rolled and most end in a teat, which catches the semen. To put a condom on:

- Expel the air from the teat at the tip of the condom by squeezing it.
- Place the opening of the condom on the penis head.
- Unroll it down the shaft to fit comfortably.

When fully unrolled, the condom should extend almost to the base of the penis and fit like a second skin, feeling silky and smooth. After ejaculation, remove the condom carefully to prevent spillage. First, the man withdraws his penis from the vagina, holding the condom securely to his penis so as not to

leave it behind. Then he removes it and disposes of it. Of course, care must be taken that any semen left on the penis does not get transferred to the woman's vagina.

Some women enjoy putting on a condom for their partner. You can use your lips or tongue to help unroll it down the penis – but be careful not to snag it with your nails or jewellery.

SEX DRIVE

Our sexuality is an important part of our individuality and our humanity. The sex drive is a creative force – it creates not only babies, but also bonds. Most relationships are initiated by sexual attraction, and while the attraction remains and sex is good, the bond will deepen. This has a biological as well as a social function, as it makes it more likely that parents will stay together to look after their offspring.

Some people have a stronger sex drive than others. It was once assumed – wrongly – that men thought about and wanted sex more than women. In reality, it varies from one individual to the next, and from relationship to relationship. Someone who has thought of themselves as passive, and not highly sexed, can get a delicious surprise when they meet a new lover with just the right chemistry. But a strong sexual need can arise for reasons other than lust – it can be triggered, for example, by insecurity. If one partner looks like straying, the other can suddenly get demonstrative in bed. Good sex is always bonding.

How often do you want sex? Some would answer: 'All the time!' Some couples make love at least once a day, even years into their relationship. Others are content with once a week, or even once a month. Remember, this is not a race or a competition. Quality is important, and feelings. Numbers don't matter, but the happiness of you and your partner does.

WHEN THE SEX DRIVE SLACKENS

When a couple begin a new relationship, their sex drive is on permanent 'go'. As the relationship progresses, especially if they are living together, the sexual needs can still be as urgent but other aspects of the relationship develop. Many people stress the need for affection and companionship as much as full-blown

sex. On average, it seems most are quite happy to make love two or three times a week, as long as there is plenty of affection as well.

When a couple have been together for many years, the sex drive may drop. This need not affect the relationship if it is a mutual occurrence. The problems begin when only one partner loses his or her usual libido level. The other partner may feel frustrated, angry, rejected and mistrust their partner's fidelity. He or she may begin to worry about their partner's health or state of mind. There can be a sense of somehow being less attractive and less worthy as a person.

Sex is a part of our lives that can often be taken for granted when going well, but when things go wrong, it looms large and affects every aspect of day-to-day living. Worries of any kind can affect the libido, from the simple immediate worry that you might be discovered by the children to health problems and career and/or financial difficulties.

Loss of libido is sometimes due to physical health problems, such as prostate complications, menopausal problems, a bad back or other debilitating illnesses. If physical health problems are not the trouble, there may be a psychological cause. Events in or outside the home that may not faze you may severely disable your partner, perhaps rendering them unable to concentrate, get an erection or become lubricated enough. At times like these, communication is crucial. If stress of some kind cannot be blamed for loss of libido, it could be a simple case of boredom. Sex for one or both of you may have become too much of a routine, following the same menu in the same place at the same time. If this is the case perhaps it's time to add a little spice to your love life.

PLAYFUL PLACES

Sensual rooms are made for sensual lovemaking. The *Kama Sutra* refers to the 'pleasure room', which says it all. If you prefer the comfort of a bed, then make your bedroom erotically appealing. Scatter luxurious cushions at the head of the bed – they could be useful for extra support. Use candles, safely dotted around the room, to give that subdued romantic feel. Burn incense or essential oils thought to have aphrodisiac properties, such as sandalwood, patchouli or ylang ylang (see pages 58–9).

The sitting room in front of a winter's fire has all the right ingredients – warmth and romantic firelight. A large, fake fur rug can be a sensory luxury for naked skin, while sofas can be useful for certain positions you might like to try. Soft pornographic videos are a safe way of discovering what each of you find, and perhaps more importantly do not find, a turn-on. Watch at the beginning as a form of titillation, or play them during your lovemaking as an erotic background. Keeping an open mind and being flexible is the key to enriching your sex life, especially when trying out different positions.

Kitchens, bathrooms, and stairways all have their own place in experimentation. They offer the additional erotic appeal of being normally unconnected with the sexual act and therefore risqué, which can be quite arousing.

Sex positions

1 Sometimes known in the East as 'split bamboo', this is a delightful way of completing a sensual body massage, or oral sex, in front of the fire.

2 The woman lies on top of the man, her whole body including her legs covering his in a 'mirror image'. During penetration, she moves herself up and down stimulating the vulva area at the same time. By closing her legs inside his spreadeagled legs, or getting him to close his inside hers, the sensation can be varied. She can also sit up quite easily from this position, stretching her legs in front of her, resting on his shoulders.

3 Beanbags and chairs have more uses than just as places to sit. They give the woman full support while the man enters her from a worshipping, kneeling position.

4 As the right height is necessary here, this position offers the pleasurable opportunity to experiment with a variety of furniture in different rooms. The woman lies on her back with her legs wide, while the man enters from a kneeling position.

Raising her legs and placing her feet on his shoulders allows the penis to be deeply 'captured' in the vagina.

5 The woman lies face-down with the man entering from the rear. By placing one or two pillows under her hips the angle of penetration can be increased. From this position, it is easy for the woman to pull herself up on all fours, or they can both roll on to their sides, while still maintaining full sexual congress.

6 Described in Hindu erotic literature as 'the deer', this rutting position is ideal for energetic sex. If penetration is too painful for the woman, she can drop down into a more gentle lying position. Some women find its animal-like quality humiliating, whereas others find it highly arousing precisely because of this connotation.

7 This position is known sometimes as 'lady's will' because, by straddling the man's lap, the woman takes full control of the movement and can delay her partner's orgasm if she wants.

8 Both partners face each other with the woman's legs over the man's to achieve penetration. By leaning backwards into a lying position, genital sensations are more concentrated since the lovers are unable to see each other.

9 Known colloquially as the 'missionary position', this is probably the most popular of all the positions. A couple can hold and kiss each other and gaze into each other's eyes while penetration takes place. It is a relaxing way, particularly for the man, to achieve orgasm after other more athletic positions have been shared.

10 In fellatio, the partner uses the lips and tongue to kiss, caress, suck and lick the penis. It is perhaps the most intimate way a woman can express her desire and love for the most masculine part of the male body, known in the *Kama Sutra* as the 'lingam'.

11 One of the most exquisite ways of achieving female orgasm is through the gentle art of cunnilingus. The wet softness of the lips and tongue are used to stimulate the clitoris in a variety of luscious ways.

12 A strenuous position that demands great neck, arm and leg strength on the part of the man. The woman holds on tightly while moving herself up and down. For the physically fit, it is a fun way to begin penetration before being lowered on to a table or a bed.

13 Known as the 'cuissade' from the French *cuisse*, meaning thigh, this is a half rear-entry position which still enables a couple to gaze upon each other and kiss face to face. The woman rests her raised leg on the man's body, while he enters 'secretly' from under her thigh.

14 Known in the *Kama Sutra* as the 'yawning position', the woman lies on her back, resting her legs on the man's shoulders. Raising the woman's buttocks with the use of cushions increases the depth of penetration. Another variation in the *Kama Sutra* is the 'pressing position'. This involves lowering the woman's legs and bending them in front of the man's chest.

15 Use the support of a wall or firmly closed door when an urgent need for each other becomes overwhelming. Penetration is achieved by the woman raising a leg coquettishly around the man.

16 This position is known in China and Japan as 'mandarin ducks', in India as the 'cobra' and in the West as 'spoons'. It has long been popular with partners whose weight creates problems, and is also useful during pregnancy. Both partners lie on their sides with the man entering from the rear.

17 In this position, the woman is definitely in control. Some men like the idea of being 'taken' while they remain helpless with their hands tied. A blindfold can add a little to the game, as the loss of sight tends to heighten the sense of touch.

18 After washing each other in a cosy bathroom, what could be more natural than fast, steamy sex? By thrusting against one another, sexual momentum builds up quickly to a crescendo.

19 A half-way position that can begin the sexual sequence or facilitate a change from one position to another, without breaking contact. Here, the woman can deepen the man's thrust by folding her leg around him, drawing him even closer.

20 The man lies diagonally across the woman, as he penetrates her. Gentle rocking from side to side builds up a delicious sexual rhythm.

21 The woman lies on her back on the bed and the man sits gently astride her, facing towards her feet. She reaches forwards to masturbate him, while he masturbates her. Because neither partner can see the other's face, this position offers total concentration on sensation alone. Before starting, the man may enjoy inserting 'love eggs' in the vagina to give the woman extra sensation.

TANTRIC SEX

Tantra comes from two ancient Sanskrit words meaning expansion and liberation. It is a form of Buddhist and Hindu teaching that sees sex as a way of expanding and exploring spirituality. The idea is that by involving your whole being in a sexual union without guilt, pleasure turns to bliss and energizes the whole of your life, bringing radiance and healing. Sexual energy, as many people can testify, has the power to transform your life, make you happy and give you confidence and self-esteem. Tantra is a philosophy of wholeness and oneness in which the man is advised to explore his feminine side and the woman to explore her masculine qualities. Both partners are encouraged to keep physically *aware* and healthy, and to meditate together. In the achievement-oriented West, orgasm is seen as the goal of sex, particularly by men. In Tantra, female satisfaction and orgasm are very important, but male orgasm should be delayed so that bliss can be prolonged. The journey is all, and after arrival, the journey is over. Men get exhausted by ejaculation, so Tantrists learn to orgasm without ejaculating. Men who practise Tantric sex can have multiple orgasms and whole-body orgasms like women.

TECHNIQUES

There are several ways a man can make his erection subside and delay ejaculation:

- Stay completely still, relax the genital and anal muscles and press your tongue against the roof of your mouth just behind your teeth.
- Stay still and take deep, regular breaths.
- Withdraw your penis a little until the urgency passes, then alternate nine shallow thrusts with one deeper one.
- Press the index finger and thumb on your perineum, midway between anus and scrotum. You or your partner can do this.
- Use the squeeze technique developed by the sexologists Masters and Johnson. Place the thumb on the frenulum (on the underside of the penis), with the index and middle fingers on the ridge of the glans on the upper side of the penis, and squeeze for 15 seconds. Either you or your partner can do this.

MASSAGE

In most Western cultures, massage is still thought of as being 'alternative'. Yet massage is the norm in the many societies that have a holistic philosophy of life – mind, body and spirit all acting as one. In such communities, touch is the essence of life. Indeed, it has been scientifically proven that tactile stimulation of a pleasurable kind releases hormones – endorphins – which promote a sense of wellbeing and aid recovery from illness. Massage relieves stress and muscle tension. It is a powerful overall mind and body therapy. If being massaged by a qualified practitioner can do all this, think about the mind-blowing possibilities of being massaged by a lover – someone who knows your body intimately who can touch parts others cannot reach? Preparations for massage are simple, but should be carried out with careful thought.

WHERE

The bedroom is the ideal place for massage, but most modern beds are too soft. The Japanese futon is perfect, but the floor is a good substitute. Use a folded blanket for cushioning, covered with a large absorbent towel.

The room should be comfortable, suitably warm and softly lit – candlelight is an added bonus. Candles can be scented or used in conjunction with burning incense or fragrant essential oils (see pages 58–9) to give an exotic atmosphere if this appeals. Gentle music which has been recorded to play for a long time without drama or interruption, is ideal for setting a tranquil mood. Ensure that you will have complete privacy for the duration of the massage and unplug the telephone, unless you have an answer machine that does not boom the caller's voice across the room as it records.

WHAT

Extra towels may be needed for covering parts of the body not being massaged, to maintain body temperature. It is surprising how quickly the body loses excess heat, especially when relaxed. Oil allows the hands to glide over the skin without friction. Ordinary vegetable oil is perfectly adequate, but you will find more luxurious massage oils in most major pharmacies. These can be used on their own or have the addition of a few drops of an essential oil. When added to a carrier oil and used in massage, essential oils give an extra boost to stimulation and relaxation, and many offer aphrodisiac properties (see pages 100–1 for some of the oils recommended for massage). Never apply essential oils directly to the skin, since they can cause severe irritation and burning.

GETTING READY

A luxurious bath is always preferable before a massage. Try sharing a bath and washing each other, but keep arousal under control. This will increase anticipation of what might become a full-blown sexual conclusion to the massage.

- Place oils in a safe place nearby where they won't be knocked over. Before applying oil to the body, always warm it in your hands first. Cold oil is never sensual.
- Make sure your lover is lying face down in a relaxed position. Before you begin, 'centre' yourself. Create a space to allow the energy, or sacred breath of life (yogis call this prana), to flow through the body into the fingertips. Breathe in deeply through the nose. Hold your breath for a few seconds, then exhale through the mouth. Try to exhale for double the time of the inhalation. Do this three times, but no longer – if you are unused to yogi breathing, it could make you dizzy. Try to put all mundane and irritating thoughts out of your mind.
- Relax the hands and wrists by shaking them. Kneel by your lover's side and, with a straight back, move from the pelvis and begin the massage.

MASSAGE STROKES

There are several different types of strokes used in massage. Tapotement, or the 'chopping' and 'striking' of the body with the hands, is perhaps what most people think of first, but for a sensual massage use the following three:

- Effleurage is a long flowing stroke, useful when applying oil. The hands stroke the body slowly and gently with an even pressure. It is a relaxing way to begin a massage.
- Petrissage, or skin rolling, is a rhythmic pulling up of the skin

and squeezing. Contrary to its description, it can be very sensual if done properly.

- Kneading is used to apply friction with the palms of the hands. It is especially good for relaxing the muscles of the limbs. The thumbs and fingers are used to concentrate on smaller areas of knotted tension.

ESSENTIAL OILS FOR MASSAGE

Essential oils must be used with care. Never increase the recommended amounts, since this could have a reverse effect or even be toxic. It is advisable to carry out a skin test prior to using any essential oil, since not all oils agree with everyone. Oils should not be used in the first three months of pregnancy, and only used in the later months after consulting a doctor.

RELAXING OILS

Type	Uses and properties	Method
Rose	Emotional soother Good for dry skin Aphrodisiac	Body & facial massage In bath
Lavender	Soporific Good for most skin types	Body & facial massage In bath
Camomile	Good for dry, sensitive skins Soothing	Body & facial massage In bath
Ylang ylang	Emotional soother Softens skin Aphrodisiac	Body massage In bath
Neroli	Stress buster Skin conditioner	Body & facial massage
Rosemary	Nerve soother	In bath

STIMULATING OILS

Type	Uses and properties	Method
Frankincense	Aphrodisiac	Body massage In bath
Patchouli	Conditions skin Aphrodisiac	Body massage In bath
Geranium	Aphrodisiac Good for oily skins Safety note: avoid sensitive skin	Body & facial massage In bath
Juniper berry	Anti-tiredness Promotes wellbeing	Body & scalp massage In bath
Bergamot	Cooling in hot weather Safety note: avoid sensitive skin	Body & facial massage In bath
Cedarwood	Soothing for itchy skin Aphrodisiac	Body & facial massage In bath
Cinnamon	Stimulating Aphrodisiac Safety note: dilute well	Body massage

MASSAGING THE BACK

- Begin to apply the oil. Use the effleurage technique, massaging from the lower back either side of the spine towards the shoulders. Push your hands in one sensual movement, following the natural contours. Lean forwards as the hands move further up.
- Move both hands outwards across each shoulder, then using your fingers, lightly slide down to rest in the starting position. Repeat this several times, moving further away from the spine towards the sides each time.
- Increase the pressure with a kneading rhythm. Use the heels of the hands as you caress upwards and give a light, smooth sweep back to the base of the spine with the flat of the hand. Rotate your finger and thumb pads on spots that feel knotty.

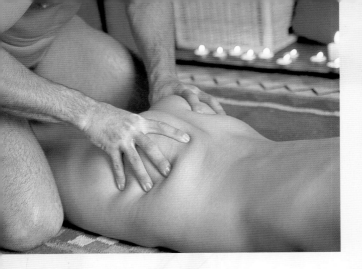

MASSAGING THE BUTTOCKS

- Begin at the top of the buttocks with fingertips touching and elbows pointing outwards. Move down firmly, kneading deeply with the palms. Follow the contours of the buttock sides, fanning out the hands so that the wrists meet at the base of the cheeks. Hold the cheeks together.
- Begin moving upwards with a firm pressure, reversing the hand movements so that they meet at the starting point with the fingertips together again. This will have a sensual effect on the genitals.
- Finish with an effleurage movement up to the neck and back down again.

MASSAGING ARMS AND HANDS

- Begin by using long, voluptuous strokes from the shoulder to the hand.
- Hold the hand and gently tug the fingers and thumb, one by one. Slide your ring and middle finger either side of each of your partner's fingers. Turn the palm up and massage with the thumb in a circular motion.
- Circle your hand around the arm, repeating a squeeze-and-move-upwards movement. Smooth the flat of the hand down from the shoulder to the wrist. Repeat several times.
- Using petrissage, work up the arm smoothly. Brush down towards the wrist with feathery strokes. Knead all the way to the shoulder, using the thumbs. Repeat several times. Enclose the arm in both hands and slide the hands down slowly, ending with the fingertips.

MASSAGING THE CHEST AND ABDOMEN

- Begin with firm effleurage circular strokes, working across the whole chest.
- Using the heels of the hands, knead your partner's upper chest on both sides.
- Repeat effleurage strokes across the chest, then up, over and under the shoulders. Massage the underside of the shoulders with the thumbs. Draw the fingers towards you, picking up and squeezing the muscles gently but firmly. Finish with long, light strokes across the shoulders and down the chest.

MASSAGING THE LEGS AND FEET

- Using the heel of the hand, knead the arch firmly towards the heel. Return to the ball with a single firm stroke. Repeat several times.
- Circle the thumbs firmly from the heel to the toes. Rotate the ankle carefully in both directions.
- Place your hands either side of the ankle. Massage using a circular kneading movement with the fingers.
- Flex toes back and forth very gently. Finally, rotate and pull each toe individually. Slide them sensually between your fingers and let them drop loose.
- Using deep effleurage strokes, move upwards to the groin. Return to the starting point, caressing the inner leg gently. Repeat the movement, but this time up the sides of the leg.
- Knead the upper surface of the thigh firmly with the thumbs. Use the heel of one hand to knead the sides while countering the pressure by holding the leg still with the other. Repeat the movement, concentrating on the back of the thigh. The leg will have to be raised slightly as you work upwards – one hand on the top, the other underneath.

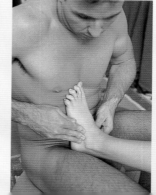

- Using petrissage, work from the inner thigh, over the top surface to the outer thigh.
- Alternately knead then pick up and roll the calf muscles with the thumbs and fingers. Finally, smooth the flats of the hands seductively down from the top of the thigh to the toes.

AQUATHERAPY

As a prelude to making love, sharing a bath or shower is delectable. It not only ensures that both partners feel beautifully fresh, but is also a bonding process. In the animal kingdom, mutual grooming is an intimacy that reinforces relationships, something that can certainly also be applied to human lovers. Soapy hands gliding all over your own or your lover's skin are a slow and delicious titillation – one of the most amorous and caring kinds of foreplay.

Add a few drops of your favourite aromatherapy oil to the bath water and soon the bathroom will be filled with an erotic

scent that cannot fail to heighten the bathtime sensual experience. Try ylang ylang, sandalwood or patchouli for a particularly heady aroma.

Using a loofah to exfoliate dead skin, followed by a cool shower, will leave you both tingling and glowing. Wash each other's hair with a scalp-stimulating shampoo such as rosemary. Use the fingertips in a circular motion to massage the scalp from the back of the neck up to the forehead and down at both sides, then rinse thoroughly.

EROTIC WATER PLAY

Match your exotically scented bodies with a little erotic play using the shower. Powerful jets of water can be a boon to tired and aching muscles, but they can also have the added bonus of sexually stimulating the nipples, clitoris and penis. Make sure that the water force and temperature is comfortable and never forcefully squirt inside the vagina, which could be harmful.

Experiment with the direction of the shower nozzle and discover what makes your lover quiver with pleasure.

Complete your pampering by smoothing on moisturizing cream and wrapping each other up in warm, fluffy towels.

Hearing

The ear is an instrument of balance, finely attuned to harmony and discord. Talking in bed offers the opportunity to tell your partner how you really feel and what you want, to share confidences as well as fantasies. But equally as important as the need to talk is the ability to listen and understand. Although men and women speak the same language they express themselves differently. This chapter explains how to increase understanding and communicate more effectively.

TALKING IN BED

Bed can be the best place of all to talk. It is a sanctuary and a
refuge, your private nest where you go to recuperate and relax.
Thoughts drift into your head and you can say just what you are
feeling into a companionable and sleepy silence. The pressure
for a structured conversation has gone. The need to organize
and be practical has slipped away with the end of the day.

Sometimes it is good to go to bed early just to talk. Have a
bath together. Then wrap yourselves in big towels and take a
drink to sip under the duvet. Propped up comfortably on
pillows side by side, it is a good time for catching up with what
has been happening and laughing over shared memories, as well
as for dreaming and planning.

Bed is a place for trust. It is not the place to make major
revelations that will upset or wound your partner. Neither is it
the place for starting a row. But it is the place for making up
once the row is over, and turning the passion of anger into sex.

TALKING THROUGH PROBLEMS

Bed can also be the place for talking calmly together about
difficult things, lying and looking into one another's eyes. It is
certainly the place for helping each other with emotional and
sexual problems. Because men can find it more difficult to talk
about love and sex, it usually falls to the woman to take the
lead. Keep it simple, keep it honest and avoid criticism, blame,
recriminations, comparisons – anything that might wound. Try
to break through your partner's inhibitions by talking first
about your own feelings, fears and inadequacies. Aim to spend
as much time listening as talking. Men sometimes need time to
become convinced that you will not think less of them for
admitting to emotions beyond their control. Don't push it. The

ego is notoriously vulnerable. If you are tempted to dent it, you
will put your cause back several steps. It is best to say just a little
to open up a sensitive subject, then to give reassurance by
snuggling up and going to sleep, rather than to hammer home
your message all in one session. A responsive partner will think
through what you have said and come up with their own ideas.
A less responsive person may need the drip-drip technique. As
long as you do it lightly and with care, avoiding a demanding
edge to your voice or a needy whine, you should be able to get
your relationship back on track.

SHARING FANTASIES

Some couples like to share sexual fantasies in bed. In an atmosphere of complete trust and acceptance, this can be highly erotic. It can break down inhibitions and increase mental and physical intimacy. It can be fun in a teasing, imaginative way. Always be aware that it is a dream world that you are dealing with. If you get upset about your partner's fantasies, and use them to fuel an argument, you will have missed the point. A sexual fantasy differs from the real-life enactment of the very same scene because there is no responsibility involved. In the fantasy, everything runs in accordance with the fantasizer's wishes. The will of the other person or people do not intrude, nor do extraneous physical sensations. The fantasizer concentrates on marrying the fluid mental picture with the exquisite sensations of building up to orgasm.

If you think you might feel threatened by your partner's fantasies, then sharing them is not a good idea. Hearing that your partner entertains lustful thoughts about your best friend or someone at work can make you angry and upset, unless you are confident that there is no desire to turn fantasy into reality. Start off if you like by exploring other people's fantasies – there are plenty of erotic books to help you get into the mood.

SLEEPING EASY

Whenever you go to bed with each other last thing at night, bear in mind the old maxim: 'Never let the sun go down on a quarrel'. We are not talking about deep and serious problems here, but everyday tiffs that if not resolved can smoulder away and grow to unreasonable proportions. Lying next to your lover, angry with something he or she has done or said that day, is not conducive to a refreshing night's sleep. Often a simple 'sorry' can break the tension and prompt an answer of 'I'm sorry too'.

TIME FOR YOURSELVES

When a couple first meet and love is in the air, they can't wait to spend time alone together. In the early stages, both may be so impatient to get to know each other that time spent apart becomes meaningless, and work commitments, family and friends are neglected.

Of course, once the relationship is well established, things will necessarily begin to change. Familiarity and routine will take the edge off excitement. The birth of a baby will shift the whole focus of a relationship. All too quickly, time alone becomes a rare event, and before the pair know it they may not even remember how to be alone together. The roles of parent and householder have swamped those of lover and confidant.

Children, grandparents, outside friends and interests, career worries, house, school and health problems can all widen the gap between them. But it doesn't have to be this way if a little thought is given to the changes that will inevitably occur with time. The key to keeping love alive is spending private time together, as often as you can.

DEMANDS OF CHILDREN

Having a baby is a time of great joy, but also a time of great change. After all the drama of even the most easy of births, the couple will never be the same again. Their roles in life have changed. Their responsibilities have doubled and their privacy halved. For a woman who is breast-feeding, those breasts that gave both lovers pleasure before now take on a new meaning and function. Some women find it very difficult to switch from being mother to lover, even when their bodies have recovered from the trauma of childbirth. Newborn babies are very demanding, feeding through the night is exhausting, but a new mother's attention has to be focused on the baby. Fathers, of course, are also affected. They too will be woken through the night. They might have worries about taking on their new financial responsibility. But above all, whereas before they were number one in their partner's life, now their physical and emotional needs usually come second.

Once the baby becomes a child, and there are perhaps additional babies in the family growing up, the demands on the parents' time and emotions are even greater. If thought has been put into adjusting to these changes, relationships can not only survive but grow closer. Just as when the parents were new lovers, privacy is of the essence.

Children brought up within the flexible constraints of a routine and who have their own privacy respected as they get older, will respond to their parents' need for privacy. This is especially important where there are step-children living at home from a previous relationship. They are likely to have been through an emotional upheaval and resent their parent spending time with a new partner.

The children's bedtime, even if they are allowed to read or play quietly in their bedroom, should be at a regular time.

They should be told that just as they have special times with their mother or their father, similarly this is their parents' special time together. Couples will benefit from spending at least part of this 'free' time exploring their relationship and keeping it alive. Talk about how you feel and how you are getting on. It is all too easy to talk about nothing except the children and family plans, but save these discussions for another time.

MAKING TIME

Plan something special at least twice a month. Book a babysitter and go out for a meal. Go to the cinema or whatever it was that you did together before the children were born. When babysitters are not available, plan an evening in. Put off visits from friends or relatives. Have a luxurious bath together and a sensual massage. Ask personal questions about thoughts and needs, and insist on personal answers. In short, take time to devote yourselves to each other and rekindle your desire.

SPEAKING THE SAME LANGUAGE?

Most relationships that fail break down because of a lack of proper communication. You may be talking to each other, but do you really understand what your partner means? Just speaking the same language with your own sex has difficulties at times; differences in socio-economic backgrounds, expectations and needs can all lead to crossed wires.

When a man and a women embark on communication, they have an additional hurdle in the form of their different genders. Inevitably, these genders have created differences in the way they were raised and in what society expects of them. In a committed relationship, both have to make an effort to understand and cross this divide, to reach a point where they are on the same wavelength.

Men often claim women are illogical, because most of their ways of looking at situations and talking about them are based on feelings. Men, on the other hand, may be accused of being unfeeling – viewing events and relationships in an overly logical way. Men often complain, too, that their partners kick up a fuss or become 'too emotional' over the slightest thing. But brushing worries under the carpet for the sake of carrying on as

normal is not always a good idea. Men often suffer from stress-related illnesses that could be avoided with a more open attitude to diagnosing and solving problems.

Perhaps one of the greatest differences between men and women is that most women do not compartmentalize their lives like most men tend to do. This may stem from the fact that women, especially those with children, often have to attend to and concentrate on several different tasks at once. They are constantly forced to 'switch hats'. Many men, on the other hand, are able to completely divorce their emotional life from their working life.

FAILING TO TALK

The basic practical differences in the way men and women run their lives spill over into the way they communicate with each other. This becomes more apparent within a long-term relationship, when partners may have given up an early attempt at equal sharing and settled down into separate roles, often along traditional lines.

'Start as you mean to go on,' is not an easy maxim to follow in a relationship that is going to grow and develop as the individuals themselves change over the years. In a balanced partnership, new developments in views on anything from social issues to sexual needs should be discussed and where applicable assimilated. It is when they are ignored that real communication problems occur.

We all know both of couples who barely ever speak to each other at all and of those who are constantly at war, verbally and sometimes physically. Neither situation is healthy, although verbal warfare is perhaps preferable to a silent relationship, if only because there is a glimmer of a chance that one day what is being shouted will eventually be heard and listened to by the other partner. Silence offers no such chance. Living with someone for any length of time does not automatically endow mind-reading ability. If a relationship is to be emotionally fulfilling, grievances – no matter how small – must be aired, and the earlier the better before they grow out of proportion.

RAISING ISSUES

If an issue is discussed at the stage of disapproval or dislike, it stands a chance of being talked through – and heard – in a sensible, non-emotional way. It is not a good idea to suppress something purely because raising it is likely to hurt or cause an argument. A suppressed complaint affects the way we behave to our partner, and if it is suddenly released in a burst of temper, it is often accompanied by a host of other issues that are neither relevant nor perhaps even true. This does not make for an easy resolution to happen.

In a partnership, whatever is important or necessary to one partner must have an effect – albeit sometimes indirectly – on the other. Nowhere is this more significant than in the realms of sex. Someone – more often a woman rather than a man – who has no qualms about making important decisions and taking action in most areas of his or her life may still balk at asking for a new aspect of sexual attention that they long for, especially if their partner has never shown any desire in that direction. There is no place for faintheartedness or embarrassment in a loving bed. Who knows, once an individual has made the suggestion, they may find that their partner has been thinking along the same lines, but was similarly fearful of mentioning it.

TRAPPED BY THE STATUS QUO

There is sometimes a feeling that two people have rubbed along together quite nicely without any major upheavals, so why rock the boat? If 'rubbing along together' is all that a couple want from a relationship, then why indeed.

However, some people find change a challenge, a welcome stimulation in an everyday existence. Some people positively need to instigate change in order to keep going. Others hate it. They feel any change is an unquestionable nightmare to be avoided whenever possible.

If your partner hates change and you are the one who wants to introduce a new element that will have a great effect on your relationship, you certainly have to work on your communication skills. And it will be worth it.

INDEX

126

ACKNOWLEDGEMENTS

Executive Editor **Jane McIntosh**
Editor **Sharon Ashman**
Executive Art Editor **Leigh Jones**
Production Manager **Louise Hall**
Picture Researcher **Jennifer Veall**

All photography © **Octopus
    Publishing Group Ltd/ Colin
    Gotts**